AF228592

THE WORLD'S FASTEST
PLANES

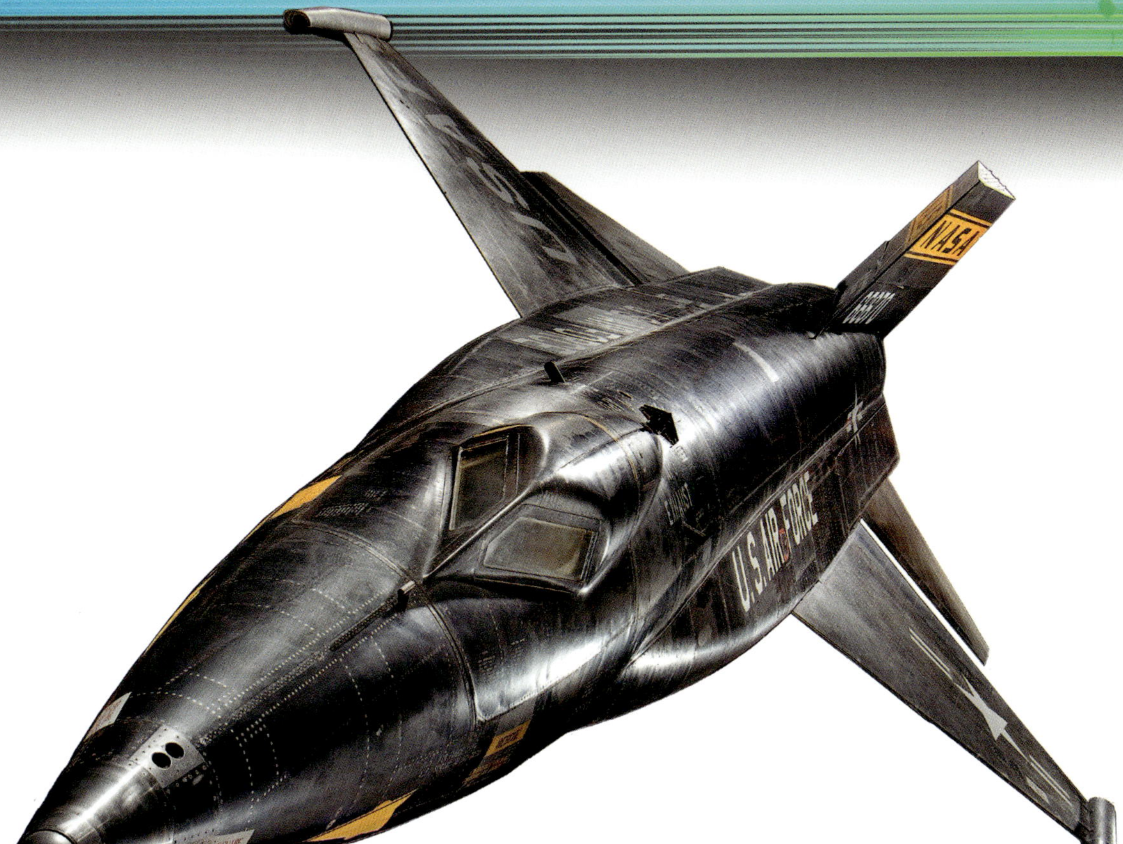

A&D Xtreme
BOLD HI-LO NONFICTION

An imprint of Abdo Publishing
abdobooks.com

S.L. HAMILTON

ABDOBOOKS.COM

Published by Abdo Publishing, a division of ABDO, PO Box 398166, Minneapolis, Minnesota 55439. Copyright © 2021 by Abdo Consulting Group, Inc. International copyrights reserved in all countries. No part of this book may be reproduced in any form without written permission from the publisher. A&D Xtreme™ is a trademark and logo of Abdo Publishing.

Printed in the United States of America, North Mankato, MN.

042020
092020

Editor: John Hamilton; Copy Editor: Bridget O'Brien

Graphic Design: Sue Hamilton; Imprint Template Design: Dorothy Toth

Cover Design: Victoria Bates

Cover Photo: US Air Force

Interior Photos & Illustrations: Alamy-pgs 16-17; Alan Wilson-pgs 20-21; AP-pgs 8, 26-27 & 32-33; Boeing-pgs 28-29; Boom Technology-pg 44; Daher-pg 18; GE Aviation-pgs 10-11; Getty-pgs 34-35; Gulfstream Aerospace-pg 31 (inset); History in Full Color-pg 6; IFR Magazine-pg 9; iStock-pg 9 (background); NASA-pgs 4-5, 17 (inset), 38-39, 40-41 & 42-43; Pilatus-pg 19; Shutterstock-pgs 12-13 & 36-37; Smithsonian Institute-pg 1; Solar Flight-pgs 14-15; SyberJet-pgs 24-25; Textron Aviation-pgs 30-31; Tim O'Brien-pgs 22-23; US Air Force-pg 7.

LIBRARY OF CONGRESS CONTROL NUMBER: 2019956096

PUBLISHER'S CATALOGING-IN-PUBLICATION DATA

Names: Hamilton, S.L., author.

Title: The world fastest's planes / by S.L. Hamilton

Description: Minneapolis, Minnesota : Abdo Publishing, 2021 | Series: Xtreme speed | Includes online resources and index

Identifiers: ISBN 9781532193941 (lib. bdg.) | ISBN 9781098212728 (ebook)

Subjects: LCSH: Speed--Juvenile literature. | High-speed aeronautics--Juvenile literature. | Motor vehicles--Juvenile literature. | Transportation--Juvenile literature.

Classification: DDC 629.046--dc23

TABLE OF CONTENTS

THE WORLD'S FASTEST PLANES

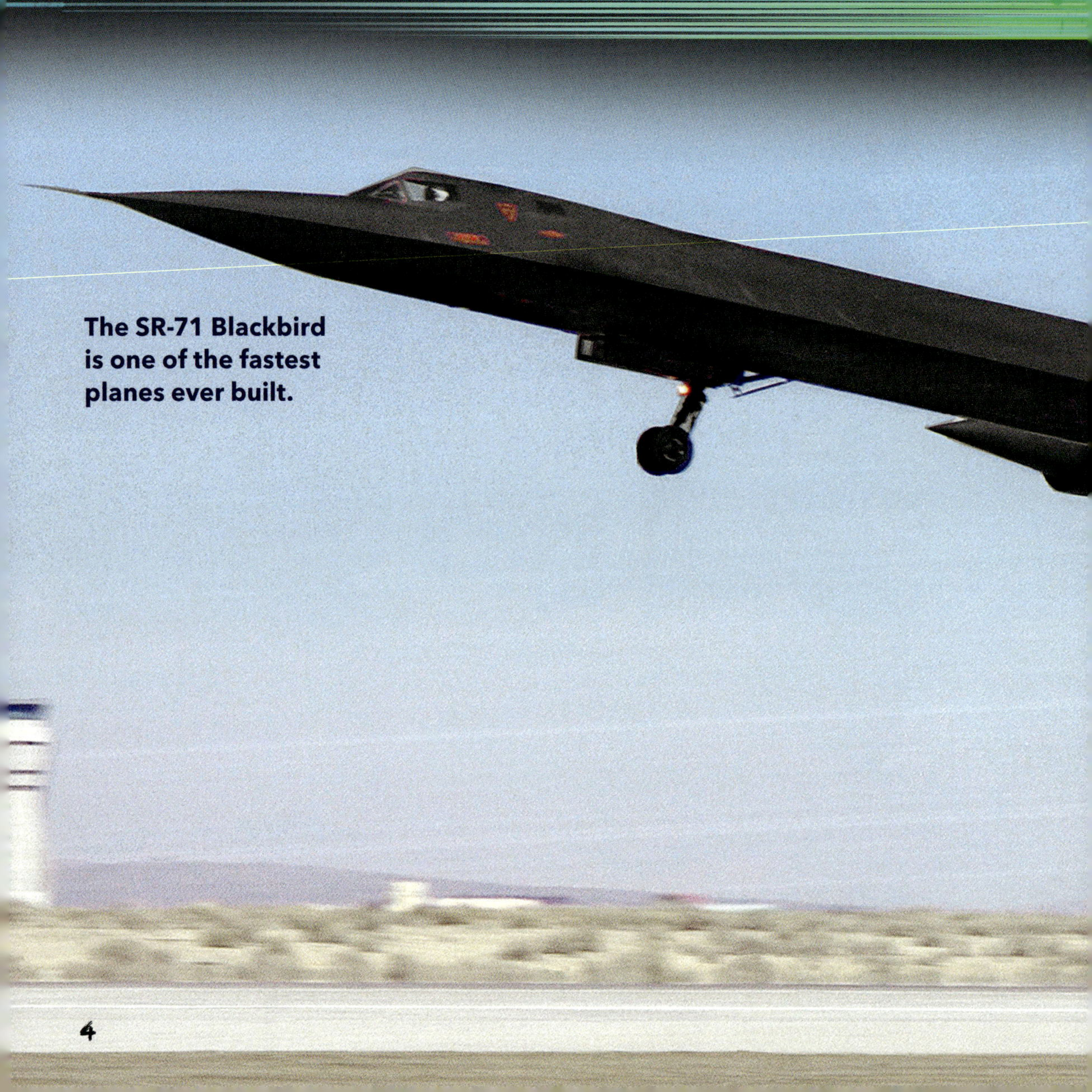

The SR-71 Blackbird is one of the fastest planes ever built.

The world's fastest planes depend on an **aerodynamic** shape and the skilled knowledge of engineers and pilots. Fighting the forces of gravity, the fastest planes are a blur of sound and color in the sky above.

CHAPTER 2

HISTORY

Airplane designs were found in Greece as far back as 400 BC. In 1502, Italian Leonardo da Vinci studied birds and designed an aircraft. Gliders were developed in the mid- and late-1800s. Orville and Wilbur Wright made the first controlled flights of a powered airplane on December 17, 1903, in North Carolina.

Orville Wright pilots the *Wright Flyer I* while brother Wilbur runs at the wingtip. The first flight lasted 12 seconds and covered 120 feet (37 m).

Chuck Yeager broke the sound barrier in a Bell X-1 named *Glamorous Glennis*, after his wife.

Airplanes were used to photograph the enemy during World War I. Jet engines were first developed in 1937. US Air Force pilot Chuck Yeager was the first to go faster than the **speed of sound** in a Bell X-1 on October 14, 1947. Later in the 20th century, even faster aircraft were developed for the military. **Civilian** aircraft soon followed, moving passengers and freight as quickly as possible.

CHAPTER 3

PILOTS

A person must pass a medical exam, have 2 months of ground training, and complete at least 40 hours of flight experience to become a licensed pilot. Most people first earn a private pilot's license for flying a single-engine plane.

A person can take flying lessons at any age, but must be 16-17 years old to become a licensed pilot.

Advanced pilots have instrument training so they can fly in all types of weather. To become a **commercial pilot** and be paid to fly, a person must have additional ground training and flight hours.

CHAPTER 4

ENGINES

Aircraft engines grew as the size of planes grew. However, oversized engines cause too much wind **drag**. Aircraft engines are properly sized to give the maximum power and the least amount of drag possible.

An engineer works on the GE4, a supersonic passenger jet's engine that was 27 feet (8 m) long.

SPEED BEASTS

No pilot's license or training is needed to operate an ultralight, but only daylight flying is allowed.

The fastest ultralight plane reaches a top speed of 63 mph (101 kph). To be called an "ultralight" in the United States, a plane must weigh less than 155 pounds (70 kg) and can have only one seat. Most ultralights come in kits and are built by the owners.

The fastest solar-powered two-seater plane is the Sunseeker Duo. The plane's power comes from the Sun or from energy stored in batteries. It flies at an airspeed of 40 mph (64 kph), but may glide on the wind at a rate of up to 85 mph (137 kph).

XTREME FACT

Unlike most planes, the Sunseeker Duo is quiet. The pilot and passenger can speak to each other without headphones. They can even open a window!

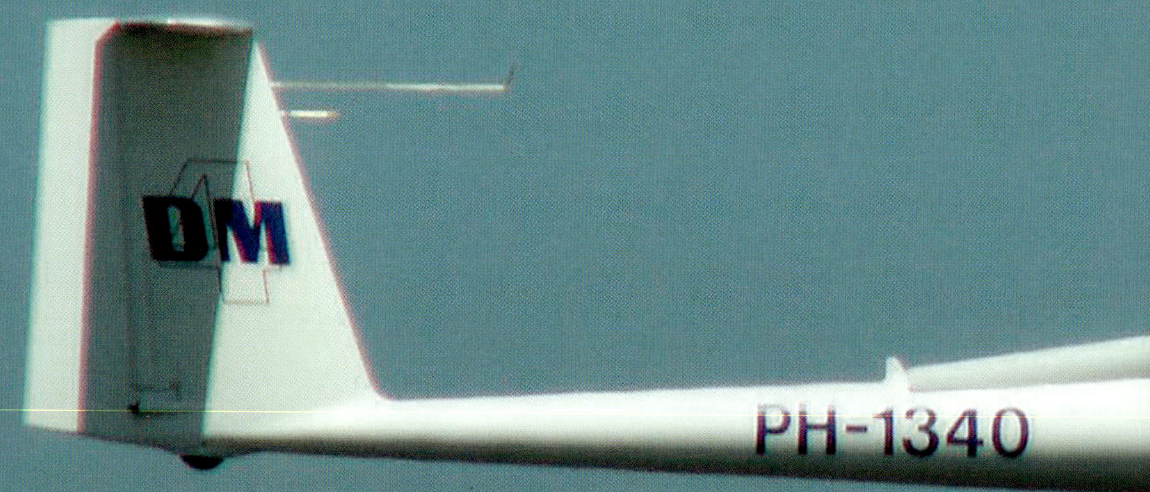

The fastest two-seat **glider** is Shemp-Hirth's Nimbus-4DM. It has a maximum airspeed of 177 mph (285 kph). The glider is sometimes called a **sailplane**.

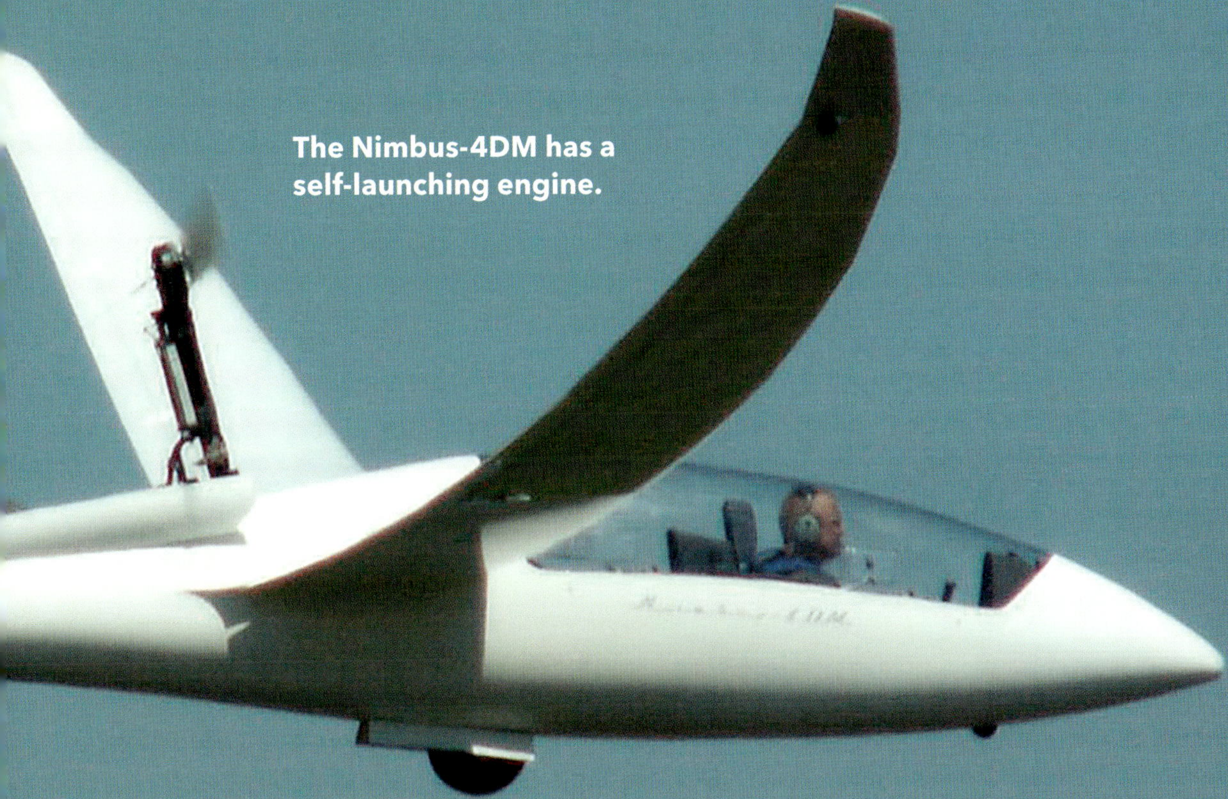

The Nimbus-4DM has a self-launching engine.

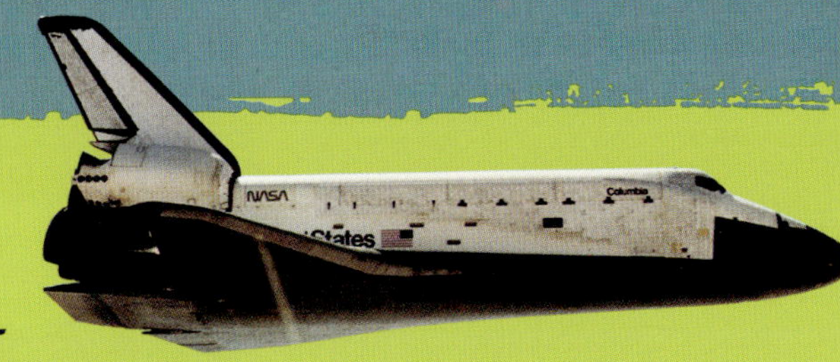

XTREME FACT

Some people say the fastest manned gliders were NASA's space shuttles. They reached 17,500 mph (28,164 kph) after re-entry into Earth's atmosphere.

CHAPTER 6

SPEED MONSTERS

The fastest **civilian** single-engine **turboprop** plane is Daher's TBM 900. The French plane's top speed is 380 mph (611 kph).

The TBM 900 can go faster than some small jets.

The fastest military single-engine **turboprop** is the Pilatus PC-21. The Swiss aircraft travels at a maximum speed of 426 mph (685 kph). It is used to train pilots.

Italy's Macchi M.C. 72 holds the world speed record for seaplanes. On October 23, 1934, test pilot Francesco Agello took the plane up to a speed of 441 mph (709 kph). This seaplane record stands today.

XTREME FACT

The Macchi M.C. 72 was the fastest aircraft of any kind from 1934-1939.

The Macchi M.C. 72 that took the world speed record is on display at the Italian Air Force Museum near Rome, Italy.

Stunt planes fly fast and make abrupt twists and turns. Pilot and air racer Lyle Shelton flew *Rare Bear*, a modified Grumman F8F Bearcat, to a record-setting speed of 528 mph (850 kph) on an aircraft course.

XTREME FACT

Pilot Steve Hinton, Jr.'s *Voodoo*, a P-51 Mustang, beat *Rare Bear's* time with a run of 532 mph (856 kph). But to set a record, speeds are averaged in four runs and must be faster by at least 1 percent. Because of this, *Rare Bear's* record stands.

Rare Bear's speed record was set at the National Championship Air Races in Reno, Nevada, on August 21, 1989.

XTREME FACT

The SyberJet SJ30 can travel across
the United States on one tank of gas.

The fastest light jet is the SyberJet SJ30. This 6-passenger aircraft has a top cruising speed of 556 mph (895 kph). It can fly nonstop for 2,877 miles (4,630 km).

The B747 Supertanker held about 20,000 gallons (75,708 liters) of water or fire retardant liquid.

Evergreen Aviation's B747 Supertanker was the biggest and fastest firefighting aircraft. It flew at a top speed of 600 mph (966 kph). The huge plane held eight times as much water or **fire retardant** as regular airtankers. In 2017, it was replaced by a Global 747-400 Supertanker, with similar abilities.

XTREME FACT
Boeing 747-8i's are planned to replace
the current US president's Air Force One
and vice president's Air Force Two.

The fastest wide-body passenger airliner is the Boeing 747-8i. It holds 467 passengers and speeds through the air at 659 mph (1,061 kph). The Boeing 747-8i is the largest commercial aircraft built in the United States.

Textron Aviation's Citation X+ (pronounced "Ten Plus") is the fastest business jet (bizjet). It can travel at a top speed of 717 mph (1,154 kph), around the **speed of sound**. It carries up to 12 passengers.

XTREME FACT

The Citation X+ took the "fastest bizjet" title from the Gulfstream G650.

CHAPTER 7

SPEED DEMONS

Air France and British Airways' Concorde was the first and fastest **supersonic** passenger aircraft. With a top speed of 1,354 mph (2,179 kph), a Concorde could travel between London and New York in about 3 hours. It takes more than 7 hours with a regular jet.

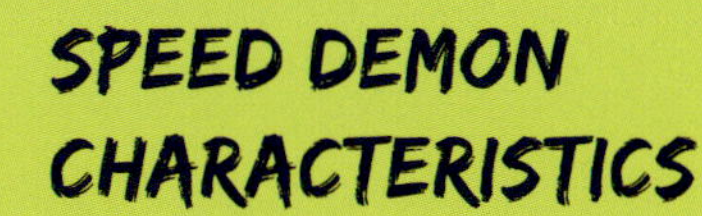

SPEED DEMON CHARACTERISTICS

TOP SPEED RANGE
1,354-2,171 mph
(2,179-3,494 kph)

SPEED DEMON TYPES
Supersonic Passenger Jet,
Supersonic Cargo Plane,
Supersonic Military Jet

A Concorde traveled at more than twice the speed of sound.

Cargo planes vary by size and weight. The fastest was the Tupolev Tu-144D. The Russian freight-only plane had turbojet engines. Its top cruising speed was 1,650 mph (2,655 kph). It flew from 1979-1983.

XTREME FACT

The "D" in Tupolev Tu-144D
stood for the Russian word
dal'nyaya or "long range."

The Soviet MiG-25 Foxbat is a **supersonic** military plane with a top speed of 2,171 mph (3,494 kph). Equipped with four missiles and powerful radar, the jet is used as a spy aircraft or an **interceptor**.

XTREME FACT

From 1965-1977, the MiG-25 Foxbat
earned 29 aviation records, including
a world speed record in 1965.

SPEED FREAKS

The Lockheed YF-12 was an American **interceptor** plane. Only three were built in the early 1960s. The jet fighter beat speed and **altitude** records at the time. Its top speed was 2,275 mph (3,661 kph). Its highest altitude record was more than 80,000 feet (24,384 m).

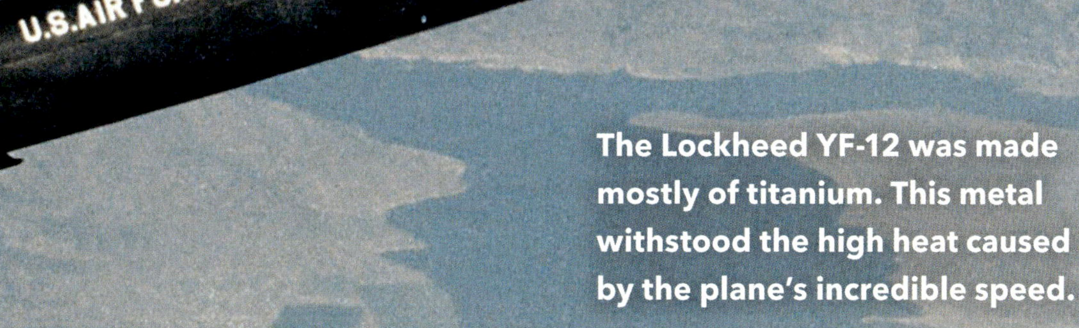

The Lockheed YF-12 was made mostly of titanium. This metal withstood the high heat caused by the plane's incredible speed.

Lockheed's SR-71 Blackbird holds the world record as the fastest piloted **supersonic** spy aircraft. The plane holds the non-rocket-powered speed record of 2,547 mph (4,099 kph). It is so fast it outruns surface-to-air missiles!

XTREME FACT

The SR-71 Blackbird is nicknamed "Habu." When it flew from an air base in Okinawa, Japan, local people thought it looked like a native habu pit viper.

The North American X-15 holds the record as the fastest, piloted, rocket-powered aircraft. Pilot Pete Knight took the X-15 to the **hypersonic** speed of 4,520 mph (7,274 kph) on October 3, 1967.

XTREME FACT

The X-15 paved the way for NASA's space shuttles. It proved that an aircraft could re-enter the atmosphere and come to a precision landing on the ground.

The "edge of space" is an **altitude** of about 62.1 miles (100 km). Pilot Joe Walker took the X-15 even higher. He reached a record altitude of 67 miles (108 km) on August 22, 1963. The X-15's speed and altitude records remain today.

The rocket-powered X-15 bridged the gap between flight in Earth's atmosphere and flight into space.

CHAPTER 9

FUTURE CONCEPTS

Planes similar to the Concorde and Tupolev Tu-144D may once again transport people and cargo at **supersonic** speeds. Boom Technology's XB-1 may fly passengers at speeds of 1,452 mph (2,337 kph). Boeing is working on a **hypersonic** plane. It would cruise at 3,800 mph (6,116 kph)!

XTREME CHALLENGE

TAKE THE QUIZ BELOW AND PUT WHAT YOU'VE LEARNED TO THE TEST!

1) Who was the first person to fly faster than the speed of sound? How fast was he going?

2) What is the youngest age that someone can get a private pilot's license?

3) How does someone become a commercial pilot?

4) What was the first supersonic passenger jet? What was the first supersonic cargo jet?

5) What is the fastest piloted aircraft? Who flew it and how fast did it go?

6) What altitude is considered the "edge of space?"

7) How fast is supersonic speed? How fast is hypersonic speed?

GLOSSARY

aerodynamic – A smooth, streamlined shape that reduces the drag, or resistance, of air moving across its surface. Planes with aerodynamic shapes go faster because they don't have to push as hard to get through the air.

altitude – The height of an object above sea or ground level.

civilian – Someone who is *not* a member of the military, police, or fire department. A nonmilitary person.

commercial pilot – A person who charges money for their work as a pilot, such as flying sightseeing tours, transporting cargo, being a flight instructor, or other paid flying jobs.

drag – The resistance that planes face as they push through air.

fire retardant – A combination of water, fertilizer, thickener (such as clay), and iron oxide (which gives it the red color) spread by firefighting aircraft. It keeps a fire from spreading.

glider – An engineless plane that flies by using air against its lifting surfaces. Self-launching gliders have engines for takeoff.

hypersonic – Extremely high speed between 3,821-7,643 mph (6,150-12,300 kph).

interceptor – An aircraft that flies rapidly toward another aircraft and prevents it from reaching its destination, either with a warning or by force.

sailplane – A glider designed to fly and gain altitude solely from natural forces, such as rising warm air.

speed of sound – The speed of sound waves traveling through air is about 700 mph (1,127 kph) at 43,000 feet (13,106 m), the approximate altitude in which test pilot Chuck Yeager made his historic 1947 flight. The speed of sound is also called Mach 1.

supersonic – Speeds greater than the speed of sound. The range may go from about 700-3,820 mph (1,127-6,148 kph). Speeds above that range are called hypersonic.

turboprop – An aircraft whose engine powers a propeller.

ONLINE RESOURCES

To learn more about the world's fastest planes, please visit abdobooklinks.com or scan this QR code. These links are routinely monitored and updated to provide the most current information available.

INDEX